Our Community Helpers

Teachers Help

Public Library District of Columbia

by Tami Deedrick

Consulting Editor: Gail Saunders-Smith, PhD

CAPSTONE PRESS
a capstone imprint

Pebble Books are published by Capstone Press,
1710 Roe Crest Drive, North Mankato, Minnesota 56003
www.capstonepub.com

Library of Congress Cataloging-in-Publication Data
Cataloging-in-Publication information is on file with the Library of Congress.
ISBN 978-1-4765-3949-2 (library binding)
ISBN 978-1-4765-5153-1 (paperback)
ISBN 978-1-4765-6010-6 (ebook PDF)

Note to Parents and Teachers

The Our Community Helpers set supports national social studies
standards for how groups and institutions work to meet individual
needs. This book describes and illustrates teachers. The images
support early readers in understanding the text. The repetition of
words and phrases helps early readers learn new words. This book
also introduces early readers to subject-specific vocabulary words,
which are defined in the Glossary section. Early readers may need
assistance to read some words and to use the Table of Contents,
Glossary, Read More, Internet Sites, and Index sections of the book.

Printed in the United States of America in North Mankato, Minnesota.
012015   008702R

Table of Contents

What Is a Teacher? 5

What Teachers Do 7

Tools Teachers Use 17

Teachers Help 21

Glossary 22

Read More 23

Internet Sites 23

Index 24

What Is a Teacher?

Teachers are people who help students learn new things. Teachers explain facts and ideas so students can understand them.

What Teachers Do

Teachers help students learn about subjects. Reading, writing, and art are subjects. Math and science are subjects too.

Some teachers teach many subjects. They teach reading, math, and science. Other teachers teach one subject like art or music.

Some teachers stay with one group of students all day. Other teachers teach many groups throughout the day.

Teachers plan lessons. They gather the supplies needed for the lesson.

Teachers give homework and tests. Then teachers grade the papers. Teachers check to make sure students are learning.

Tools Teachers Use

Teachers use tools to help students learn. They use books and computers to help them teach.

Other tools are important for learning. Maps and charts display information. Movies and pictures can help students see a subject more clearly.

Teachers Help

Teachers help students learn about the world. They also help students learn about themselves and each other.

Glossary

display—to show

information—facts and knowledge

science—the study of nature and the physical world by testing, doing experiments, and measuring

subject—an area of study such as reading, math, or science

Read More

Heos, Bridget. *Let's Meet a Teacher.* Community Helpers. Minneapolis: Millbrook Press, 2013.

Jeffries, Joyce. *Meet the Teacher.* People Around Town. New York: Gareth Stevens Pub., 2013.

Murray, Aaron R. *Teachers Help Us.* All About Community Helpers. Berkeley Heights, N.J.: Enslow Elementary, 2013.

Internet Sites

FactHound offers a safe, fun way to find Internet sites related to this book. All of the sites on FactHound have been researched by our staff.

Here's all you do:

Visit *www.facthound.com*

Type in this code: 9781476539492

Check out projects, games and lots more at
www.capstonekids.com

Index

books, 17
computers, 17
facts, 5
homework, 15
ideas, 5

lessons, 13
planning, 13
subjects, 7, 9, 19
tests, 15
tools, 17, 19

Word Count: 159
Grade: 1
Early-Intervention Level: 18

Editorial Credits
Erika L. Shores, editor; Gene Bentdahl, designer; Charmaine Whitman, production specialist

Photo Credits
All photos by Capstone Studio/Karon Dubke